Business LEADERS

Kristy Stark, M.A.Ed.

Publishing Credits

Rachelle Cracchiolo, M.S.Ed., *Publisher*
Conni Medina, M.A.Ed., *Managing Editor*
Nika Fabienke, Ed.D., *Series Developer*
June Kikuchi, *Content Director*
Michelle Jovin, M.A., *Associate Editor*
Courtney Roberson, *Senior Graphic Designer*

TIME and the TIME logo are registered trademarks of TIME Inc. Used under license.

Image Credits: front cover, p.1 WorldFoto/Alamy; p.4 Castleski/Shutterstock; p.7 Everett Collection/Shutterstock; p.8 Susan Montgomery/Shutterstock; p.9 Zuma Press/Alamy; p.11 Evan Agostini/ImageDirect; p.12 Martin E. Klimek/Zuma Press/Alamy; p.15 Diabluses/Shutterstock; p.17 Underwood Archives/UIG Universal Images Group/Newscom; p.18 Tim Mosenfelder/Getty Images; pp.20–21 David Paul Morris/Getty Images; p.22 Richard Koci Hernandez/KRT/Newscom; p.23 Agencia el Universal/El Universal de Mexico/Newscom; p.25 Peppinuzzo/Shutterstock; pp.26–27 bgwalker/iStock; p.29 Tom Bible/Alamy; p.30 Castleski/Shutterstock; p.33 Anne-Marie McReynolds/KRT/Newscom; p.34 Nicescene/Shutterstock; p.35 I Am Nikom/Shutterstock; p.36 ChinaFotoPress/Zuma Press/Newscom; p.39 (left) Lorenzo Ciniglio/Polaris/Newscom; p.39 (center left) catwalker/Shutterstock; p.39 (center right) Joe Seer/Shutterstock; p.39 (right) Lev Radin/Shutterstock; pp.40–41 William Regan/Zuma Press/Newscom; all other images from iStock and/or Shutterstock.

All companies, websites, and products mentioned in this book are registered trademarks of their respective owners or developers and are used in this book strictly for editorial purposes. No commercial claim to their use is made by the author or the publisher.

Library of Congress Cataloging-in-Publication Data
Names: Stark, Kristy, author.
Title: Legacy : business leaders / Kristy Stark.
Description: Huntington Beach, CA : Teacher Created Materials, [2019] | Includes index.
Identifiers: LCCN 2017055670 (print) | LCCN 2017058127 (ebook) | ISBN 9781425854874 (e-book) | ISBN 9781425850111 (pbk.).
Subjects: LCSH: Businesspeople--United States--Juvenile literature. | Business enterprises--United States--Juvenile literature.
Classification: LCC HC102.5.A2 (ebook) | LCC HC102.5.A2 S6349 2019 (print) | DDC 338.092/273--dc23
LC record available at https://lccn.loc.gov/2017055670

Teacher Created Materials

5301 Oceanus Drive
Huntington Beach, CA 92649-1030
www.tcmpub.com
ISBN 978-1-4258-5011-1
© 2019 Teacher Created Materials, Inc.

Table of Contents

Changing the World 4

Pioneers of Entertainment 6

Titans of Technology 16

Star Sellers 28

Beyond the Boardroom 40

Glossary 42

Index 44

Check It Out! 46

Try It! 47

About the Author 48

Changing the World

Imagine a typical day in your life. It might involve a smartphone or computer and probably a few Google™ searches. It likely involves a television and some cable networks. Now, imagine a day without these devices and channels. Or imagine how you would buy a new video game if Amazon® or eBay® did not exist. Luckily, thanks to many **influential** leaders, all of these things *do* exist to make our lives easier.

Industry leaders have shaped many objects and routines in our daily lives. These leaders transformed their visions into businesses, products, and ideas that have changed the world and the way people live. The world as we know it looks significantly different from the way it did just 15 to 20 years ago, due to the **innovative** men and women who have charged forward to change people's lives.

Just Google It!

Worldwide, there are over 40,000 search requests processed by Google every second! There are about 3.5 billion searches on an average day and 2 trillion searches per year.

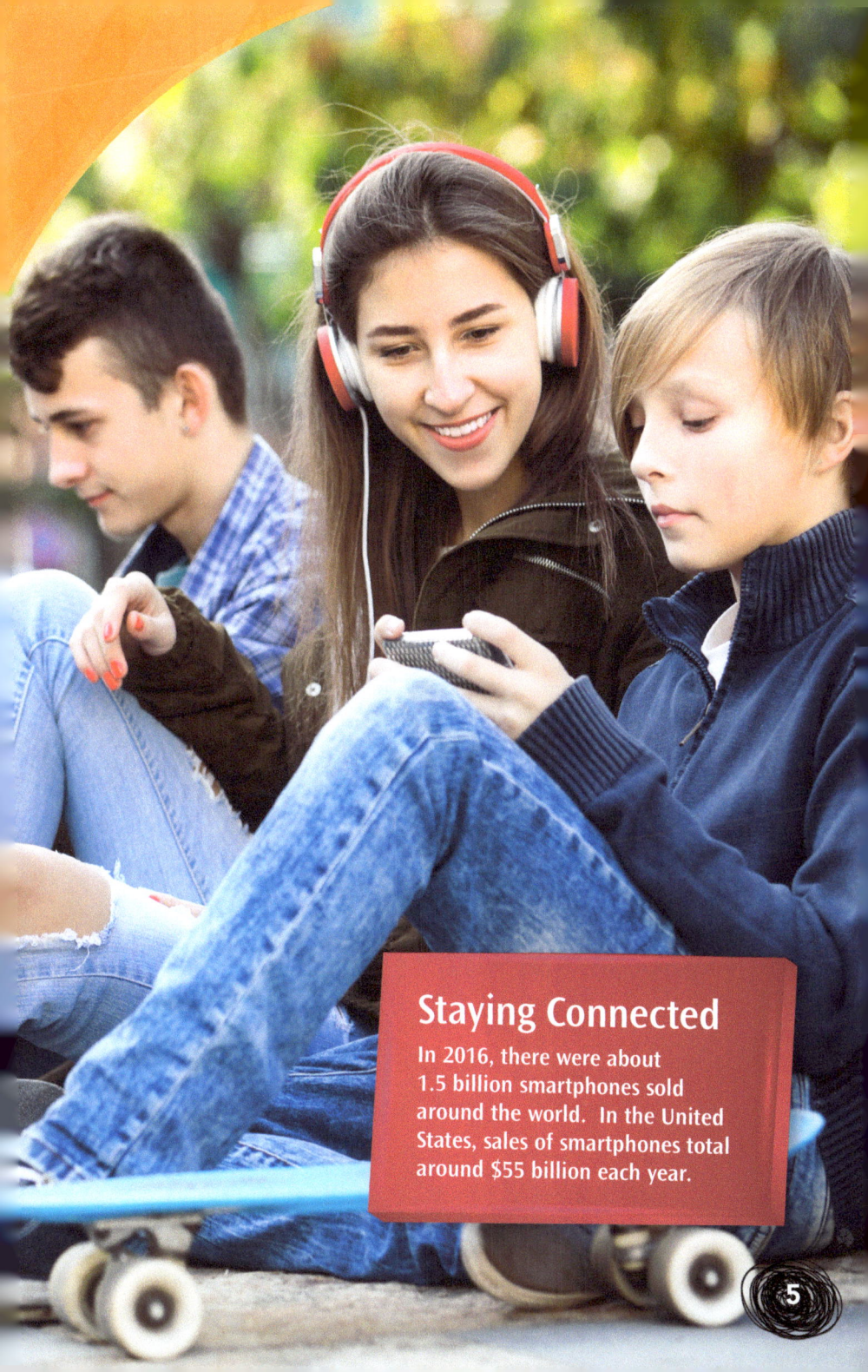

Staying Connected

In 2016, there were about 1.5 billion smartphones sold around the world. In the United States, sales of smartphones total around $55 billion each year.

Pioneers of Entertainment

TV shows and movies have been around for many years. However, the ways people watch movies and connect with TV **personalities** have drastically changed over the years.

Oprah Winfrey

Her face and name are everywhere—she is in commercials and movies, on magazine and book covers, and on TV shows. Oprah Winfrey is one of the most iconic entertainment personalities in recent history.

Winfrey started her **broadcasting** career in Nashville, Tennessee, when she was still a high school student. By the time she was 19, she was the youngest **anchor** at her news station in Nashville. Winfrey was also the first African American woman to be an anchor at that station.

In 1984, Winfrey hosted a morning talk show in Chicago. It quickly became the most watched local talk show in the city. The show was renamed *The Oprah Winfrey Show* less than a year later.

A Star Is Born

Oprah Winfrey was born in Mississippi on January 29, 1954. Her parents named her Orpah, after a woman in the Bible. That name was hard to say and spell, so everyone called her Oprah.

Oprah Winfrey

Squashing the Competition

Before Winfrey's move to Chicago, *Donahue* was the highest-rated talk show in the United States. Ratings of Winfrey's local talk show, *AM Chicago*, surpassed *Donahue* in one month after she became the host.

A Self-Made Billionaire

As of 2017, Oprah Winfrey's **net worth** was $3.1 billion. That made her one of the richest women in the United States. The richest woman, Alice Walton, is the only daughter of Sam Walton—founder of Wal-Mart.

In 1986, *The Oprah Winfrey Show* entered **syndication** in the United States. About 10 million people watched each day during the show's first year. Winfrey's show made $125 million in **gross profits** by the end of the first year. That same year, Winfrey herself made $30 million (about $66 million today).

The Oprah Winfrey Show became the highest-rated talk show in history, but Winfrey did not stop there. She started her own TV studio in 1988, which she named Harpo Studios. (*Harpo* is *Oprah* spelled backward.) She became only the third woman in the U.S. entertainment industry to create her own studio.

The Oprah Winfrey Show was on TV for 25 years. At its peak, more than 40 million people in the United States tuned in to watch each week. The show was also **licensed** to 150 countries around the world, allowing millions more to be entertained and uplifted by Winfrey.

Oprah's Book Club

Winfrey launched a book club as part of her talk show. Millions of viewers bought and read books with the "Oprah's Book Club" logo on the cover. Many unknown authors gained popularity because Winfrey selected their books for the club.

In addition to being a female **trailblazer** in entertainment, Winfrey changed the world in important ways. She tackled difficult topics on her show, and she made it her mission to help people feel connected and less alone. Winfrey prompted people to think about and discuss **sensitive** issues, such as illness, spirituality, and love.

Winfrey sought to create a show that she would be interested in as a viewer. With tens of millions of viewers, it was obvious that people connected with the show's ideas and topics. Winfrey, however, was more than just the show's host. She became a symbol of hope, change, and personal growth to people around the world.

In 2011, *The Oprah Winfrey Show* ended. In that same year, she launched her own TV channel, the Oprah Winfrey Network, or OWN. The network's mission is "to celebrate life, to inspire and entertain, **empowering** viewers around the world to live their best lives." Today, Winfrey continues to inspire people and tell stories through her life and work.

Angel Network

Winfrey formed a charity called Oprah's Angel Network in 1998. The charity has built more than 55 schools around the world and has given more than $1 million worth of school supplies to South African schools. The charity has also rebuilt almost three hundred homes in the United States that have been ruined by natural disasters.

THINK LINK

> How did Oprah's talking about sensitive issues help people feel connected and less isolated?

> If you were choosing topics for Oprah's show, which topics would you select? Why would you pick those topics?

> Oprah said she wanted to create a show that she would watch. How might that have affected decisions she made about the show?

Winfrey with the first issue of her magazine, *O*, in 2000

Reed Hastings

Blockbuster Video

The largest brick-and-mortar video rental store was Blockbuster Video. In the early 1990s, Blockbuster had almost three thousand stores around the world. It made a lot of money from late fees. In 2000 alone, the video chain charged about $800 million in late fees!

Reed Hastings

People may not be familiar with the name Reed Hastings, but they probably know the company he cofounded in 1997: Netflix. He now serves as the company's **chief executive officer** (CEO).

Hastings and Netflix forever changed the way people access movies and video games. Prior to 1997, people rented DVDs from **brick-and-mortar** video stores. These stores charged a fee to rent movies. If customers did not return the items on time, they were charged late fees. Late fees ultimately led to the creation of Netflix. Hastings was charged $40 in late fees from Blockbuster Video, and he decided that something had to change.

Netflix began as a rent-by-mail service, where users would pay a monthly fee to rent unlimited DVDs without late fees. When people finished with the DVDs, they would put them in Netflix envelopes and drop them in the mail. Then, the company would automatically send the user another DVD through the mail.

A Proposed Partnership

In 2000, Hastings attempted to form a partnership with Blockbuster Video. Blockbuster's CEO and team declined. Within 10 years, Blockbuster filed for **bankruptcy** and began to close its stores, while Netflix continued to grow and make money.

People liked the idea of not worrying about late fees, and the service quickly became popular. By 2003, Netflix had one million **subscribers**. Within two years, the number of Netflix's subscribers had more than quadrupled.

Hastings and Netflix dramatically changed the way people acquired and watched movies. Hastings was happy with his success, but he did not stop there. Netflix began to offer **on-demand streaming**. Its customers no longer needed to wait for their movies to come in the mail. Instead, people could watch movies instantly on their TVs, computers, phones, and tablets. By 2017, Netflix had nearly 100 million subscribers.

Netflix employees also began creating their own shows. Since then, Netflix's original series have been highly successful and have had hundreds of nominations for Emmy Awards, which are given to the best TV shows of the year. In 2017, Netflix won 20 Emmy Awards; the only network to win more was HBO with 29.

Changing Education

Hastings knows that many Netflix watchers are teenagers and young adults, so he works to change and shape education for them. Hastings invested money in an online program called DreamBox Learning to help students with math. He also served as the president of the California State Board of Education.

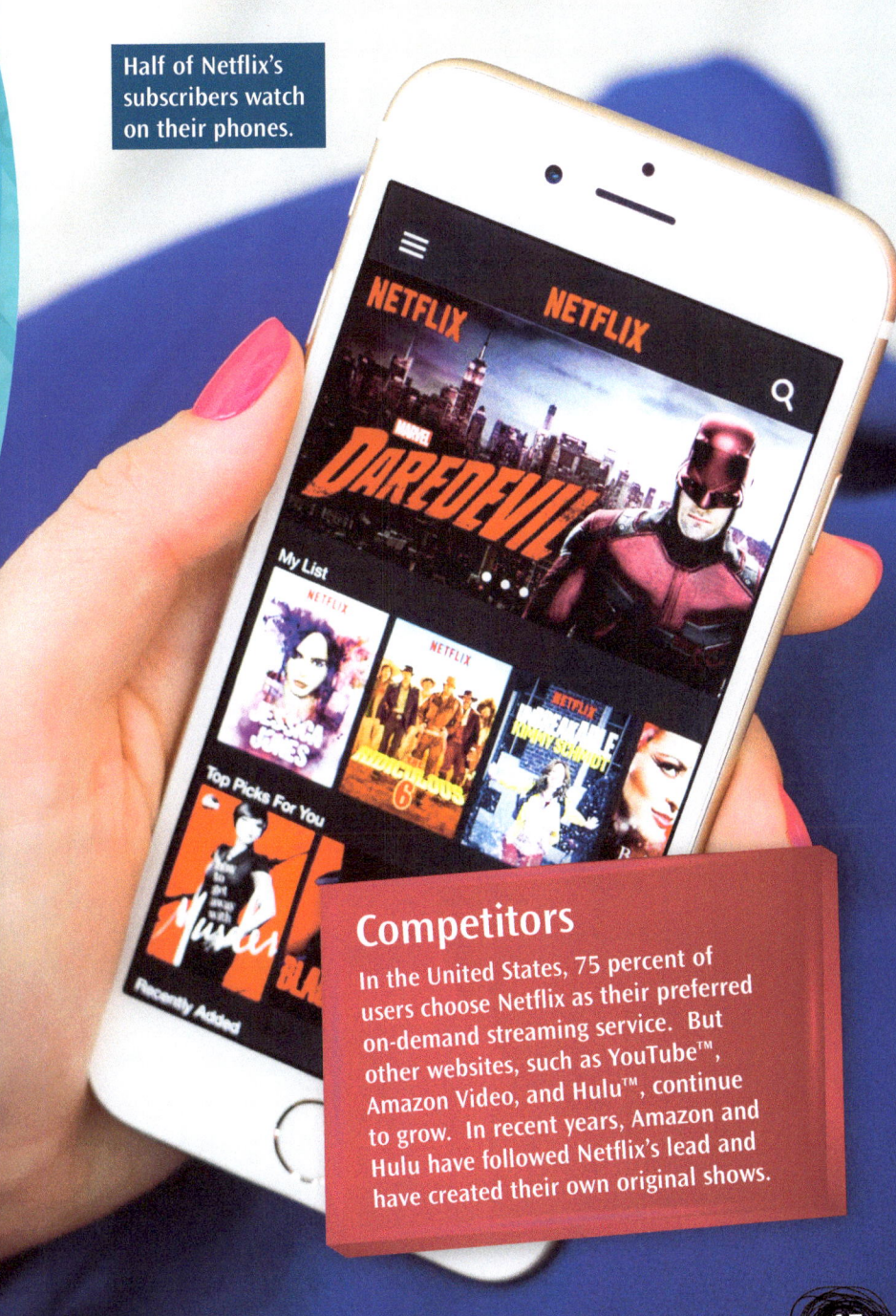

Half of Netflix's subscribers watch on their phones.

Competitors

In the United States, 75 percent of users choose Netflix as their preferred on-demand streaming service. But other websites, such as YouTube™, Amazon Video, and Hulu™, continue to grow. In recent years, Amazon and Hulu have followed Netflix's lead and have created their own original shows.

Titans of Technology

Technology changes quickly. Devices are improved, made more **efficient**, and created with new features from year to year. Countless men and women contribute to technology and its advancements every day, but there are a few brave leaders who have risked everything to create the tools that have become part of our everyday lives.

Steve Jobs

It's hard to imagine, but there was a time when having a computer in your home was almost impossible. Only giant companies, colleges, and governments had the space (and the money) for these huge machines.

Steve Jobs wanted to change this. Jobs and his friend Steve Wozniak (also known as "the Woz") started to build and sell small computers. Together, they founded Apple® Computers in 1976.

That's One Gigantic Computer!

In 1951, the first commercial computer was made in the United States. It was called the Universal Automatic Computer (or, UNIVAC for short). UNIVAC was huge—it took up almost 400 square feet (37 square meters) of floor space and weighed 29,000 pounds (13,150 kilograms)!

Two men work on the UNIVAC in 1951.

Comparing Computer Speeds

Despite its large size, the UNIVAC computer was slow. It performed 1,905 operations per second. The Apple iPad®, is almost eight hundred times smaller than the UNIVAC. It can perform 1.65 billion operations in the same amount of time!

Steve Jobs

Who's Got the Button?

Jobs frequently wore black turtlenecks to presentations, but what most people didn't know was that Jobs wore that outfit because he had a condition called *koumpounophobia*. That is the fear or dislike of buttons. That condition may seem strange to some, but it led Jobs to create the first buttonless cell phone and computer mouse.

Apple's machines were instant successes. Within just a few years, hundreds of thousands of Apple computers were sold. The creation and success of Apple I—Apple's first computer—prompted more companies to create desktop computers.

This would not be the last time that Jobs led the way toward advancements in technology. He **resigned** from Apple in 1985, but he eventually returned to the company as CEO in 1996.

When he returned, Jobs persuaded Apple to begin making electronics in addition to computers. Because the company began to make more than just computers, its name was later changed from Apple Computers to Apple Inc.

In 2001, Jobs introduced the world to the iPod®. This device could hold digital versions of music. Prior to the iPod, MP3 players existed, but they were unreliable and did not have a lot of space to store music. Jobs sought to change the way people stored, managed, and bought music.

Jobs' Other Jobs

When Jobs left Apple in 1985, he started a computer company called NeXT. He was also the owner and CEO of Pixar Animation Studios. He was in charge of Pixar when they created their first feature-length film—*Toy Story*.

End of an Era

In August 2011, Jobs resigned as CEO of Apple. He was suffering from pancreatic cancer. Jobs died on October 5, 2011, at the age of 56.

Cooking Up Something New

When Jobs stepped down as CEO, he picked Tim Cook to take his place. Cook has worked at Apple since 1998, so Jobs trusted him to lead the company into the future. Under Cook's direction, the company has introduced the Apple Watch®, Apple TV®, and Apple Pay®, as well as new advancements to the iPhone and iPad.

With the release of the iPod, Apple also launched iTunes®. For the first time, people could store and manage digital music in one place. In 2003, the iTunes Store® officially opened and sold 275,000 songs in its first day! The iTunes Store completely changed how many people bought music.

Jobs blazed his own trail once again when Apple released the first iPhone® in 2007. This phone forever changed how people used technology.

Tim Cook (left), Steve Jobs (center), and Apple's VP of Marketing Phil Schiller (right) answer questions about Apple's new products.

The iPhone was the first cell phone that also stored and played music. It was essentially a computer that fit in a person's pocket. Many companies rushed to produce cell phones that were similar, attempting to follow Jobs and Apple in the creation of this new technology.

Jobs clearly left his mark on the world through his innovative ideas and creation of new products that are still used and improved upon today.

Sergey Brin (left) and
Larry Page (right)

Backrub It

The original name of Page and Brin's search engine was Backrub. They changed the name to Google, a play on the word *googol*, which is the number 1 followed by 100 zeroes. If they didn't change the name, people might be telling others to "backrub" something instead of telling them to "google" it.

Larry Page and Sergey Brin

Similar to the way that Apple devices changed people's lives, Google changed how people search and access information. Larry Page and Sergey Brin started Google from their dorm rooms at Stanford University in California.

In 1998, the **World Wide Web** was still new. Page and Brin sought to create a search engine that would help people filter through all the information available there. Their mission was "to organize the world's information and make it universally **accessible** and useful."

At the time, Page believed that there were about 10 million documents on the web, and he wanted to figure out how these documents were connected to one another. However, Page and Brin could not do this on their own. The two men built a computer program called a *crawler*. Crawlers collect information about how websites are linked. Their crawler, now called Googlebot, is still gathering **data** for the company. The data it collects is used to constantly improve Google's search engine.

Google Doodles

Doodles are changes to the Google logo that celebrate special days or people. Google now has a team of illustrators and engineers, called *doodlers*, who design them. They have created over two thousand doodles for Google's homepages around the world.

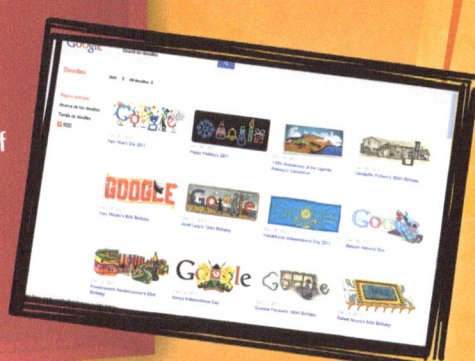

Google was not the first search engine for the web. In fact, Yahoo!® launched a year before Google. Page and Brin wanted their search engine to improve the way that all search engines worked. They did not want the search engine to just return information. In addition, they wanted the returned information to be ranked according to what was the most important and **relevant** to the search topic. To help their search engine rank the information, they created a special formula named PageRank™. It determines which search results are most important by how many pages are linked to each website.

PageRank helped make Google a popular search engine because it helped people locate the most relevant information to their searches. Today, when someone uses Google to find information, the desired information is often found within the first few search results.

Alphabet It

In 2015, Google's leaders reorganized the company. The parent company is now called Alphabet. Page is Alphabet's CEO, and Brin is its president.

a woman wears an early model of Google Glass

Google X

For several years, Brin ran a division called Google X. This department was in charge of creating Google Glass™, a computer that people could wear as eyeglasses. Google stopped production in 2015, but it is still committed to making "smart glasses" in the future.

STOP! THINK...

> What are some advantages and disadvantages of using a traditional map over Google Maps?

> What details do you notice on the bottom map that are not on the top map?

> How might getting places be different if Google Maps was never invented?

After Page and Brin's search engine became a huge success, they led Google to create other **revolutionary** programs, such as Google Maps™, which launched in 2005. This program allows users to access up-to-date images of places, directions to locations, and traffic information. Users can even view satellite images of any location taken from space.

Page and Brin did not stop there. In 2009, Google began work on self-driving cars. People in these cars can sit back and enjoy the ride. The company continues to

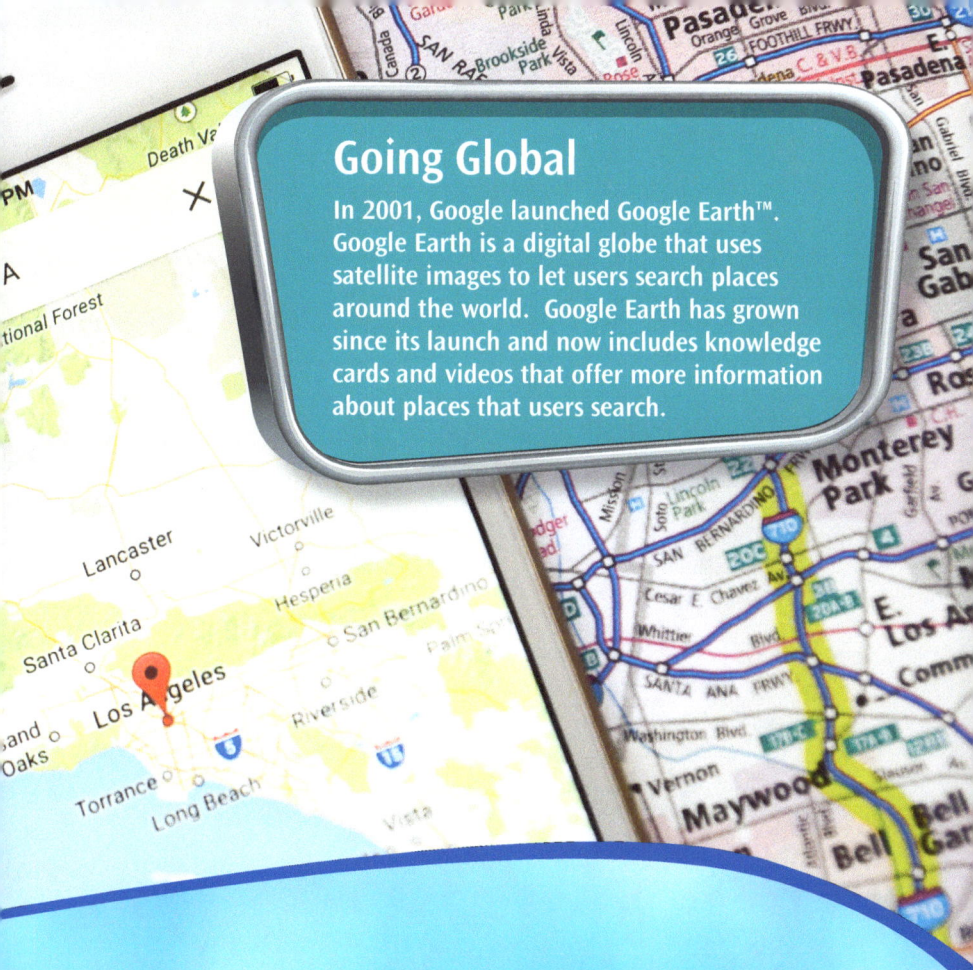

Going Global

In 2001, Google launched Google Earth™. Google Earth is a digital globe that uses satellite images to let users search places around the world. Google Earth has grown since its launch and now includes knowledge cards and videos that offer more information about places that users search.

work on testing and modifying these vehicles. By 2017, the self-driving cars had driven over three million miles (nearly five million kilometers), and were being used in select cities.

Page and Brin continue to work toward new innovations and technology. Their ideas and leadership have helped change the way people live and work.

Star Sellers

People have been buying, selling, and trading goods and services throughout history. Prior to the 1990s, however, **commerce** was done at brick-and-mortar stores, yard sales, and markets. Then, the World Wide Web was created. This new technology made it possible for people to do a lot of things, such as shop for goods, without leaving home.

Jeff Bezos

In 1986, Jeff Bezos graduated from college with degrees in both computer science and electrical engineering. Instead of pursuing a career in science, however, Bezos worked at **investment firms** on Wall Street in New York City.

Bezos used the money he made on Wall Street to develop an idea he had for an online bookstore. His bookstore started in his garage in Seattle, Washington. There, he started to develop the software for his online store. Bezos named his store Amazon, after the river in South America.

What's in a Name?

Bezos planned to call his company Cadabra (as in the word used by many magicians, *abracadabra*). His lawyer misheard the name and thought he wanted to call it Cadaver, which is a dead body. Bezos chose a different name because he did not want his company name to be mistaken for a dead body.

Jeff Bezos in 1999

A Love for Science

Although Bezos did not pursue a career in science, he loves science and has a deep interest in space travel. His other company, Blue Origin, is working to send people to space to experience what it feels like to be astronauts. The capsules will take people 62 mi. (100 km) above Earth, where passengers will experience four minutes of weightlessness.

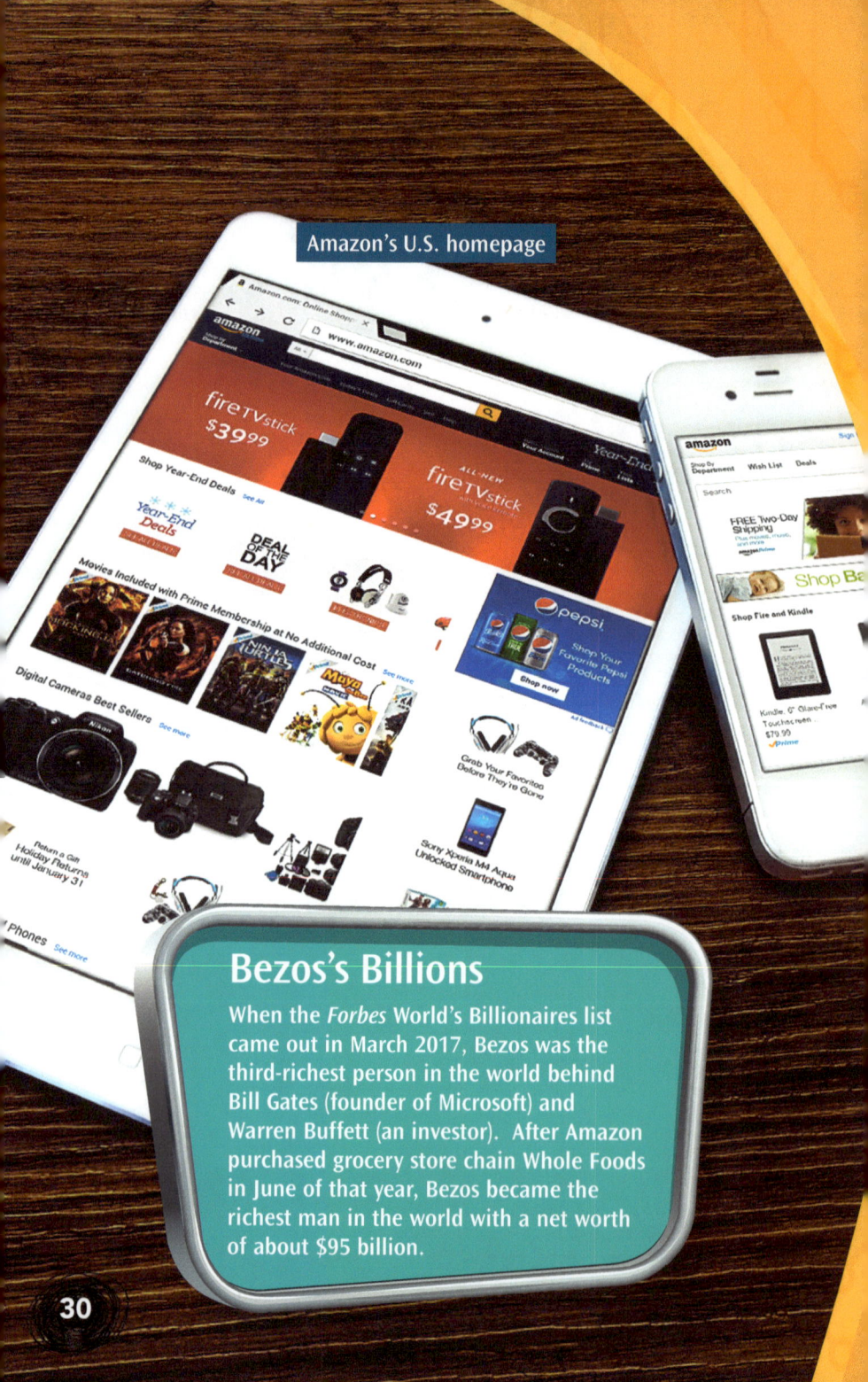

Amazon's U.S. homepage

Bezos's Billions

When the *Forbes* World's Billionaires list came out in March 2017, Bezos was the third-richest person in the world behind Bill Gates (founder of Microsoft) and Warren Buffett (an investor). After Amazon purchased grocery store chain Whole Foods in June of that year, Bezos became the richest man in the world with a net worth of about $95 billion.

Amazon opened to the public on July 16, 1995. Brick-and-mortar bookstores could only hold a certain amount of books at one time. But Amazon was completely digital, so there was no need to worry about shelf space.

Within a month after opening, Amazon was selling books in the United States and 45 other countries. By its second month, Amazon had sales of $20,000 a week. Bezos's risky idea was quickly turning into a successful business!

In 1998, Bezos decided to expand his website and sell more than books. Amazon started to sell CDs and videos, too. Bezos later added clothes, toys, gadgets, food, and more. Bezos and Amazon did not stop there. The website launched an on-demand video service in 2006. The next year, the Kindle®, a digital book reader, was released. The Kindle Fire®, Amazon's first tablet, hit the market in 2011.

The Empty Chair

One reason for Amazon's success is Bezos's belief about the importance of customers. During company meetings, Bezos has been known to purposely leave one seat empty at the table. He tells everyone to imagine that a customer, the most important person, is sitting in that seat.

In 2013, Bezos shared his ideas about using drones (unmanned aircraft guided by remote controls) to deliver packages. He is working toward using drones for Prime Air® deliveries in the coming years.

Bezos continues to look toward the future and think of new innovations for the company. That attitude has made Amazon the go-to shopping website for many people around the world. Each year, the company makes more than $130 billion.

Meg Whitman

In 1995, a new website launched, which changed how people bought and sold things. Before then, people sold their used items at yard sales or flea markets.

But Pierre Omidyar thought he could change the way business was done. He started AuctionWeb from his living room in San Jose, California. He had the idea and vision for the company, but he was not a strong manager. If he wanted his company to grow, he needed to find someone who could lead his company in the right direction.

In February 1998, Omidyar found his leader. Meg Whitman joined the newly renamed eBay as the company's president and CEO.

Beanie Baby Craze

In the 1990s, small stuffed animals called Beanie Babies were selling out at stores. People began buying them and reselling them on eBay. At the height of the craze, 6 percent of all eBay sales were Beanie Babies®.

Whitman was a great choice for the job. She had studied at Princeton University in New Jersey and Harvard University in Massachusetts. Whitman left her job as the head of Hasbro's Playskool division to go to eBay—an incredibly risky move at the time.

When Whitman took over, eBay was just getting started. It had about 30 employees and around 500,000 users. The company was earning about $5.7 million per year. Ten months later, eBay had hired over 100 new employees and had 5.6 million users. The company's earnings that year jumped to $41.7 million.

Whitman's vision for the company did not stop there. She continued to grow eBay in new ways. In 2002, eBay bought PayPal, an online payment service. Whitman explained her decision by saying, "PayPal had become the wallet on eBay. We had to own that company."

A Character Comeback

When Whitman worked at Hasbro, she was responsible for Mr. Potato Head. Mr. Potato Head was first released in 1952, making it Hasbro's oldest toy. While Whitman was in charge, Mr. Potato Head made a huge comeback after it appeared as a character in *Toy Story* in 1995.

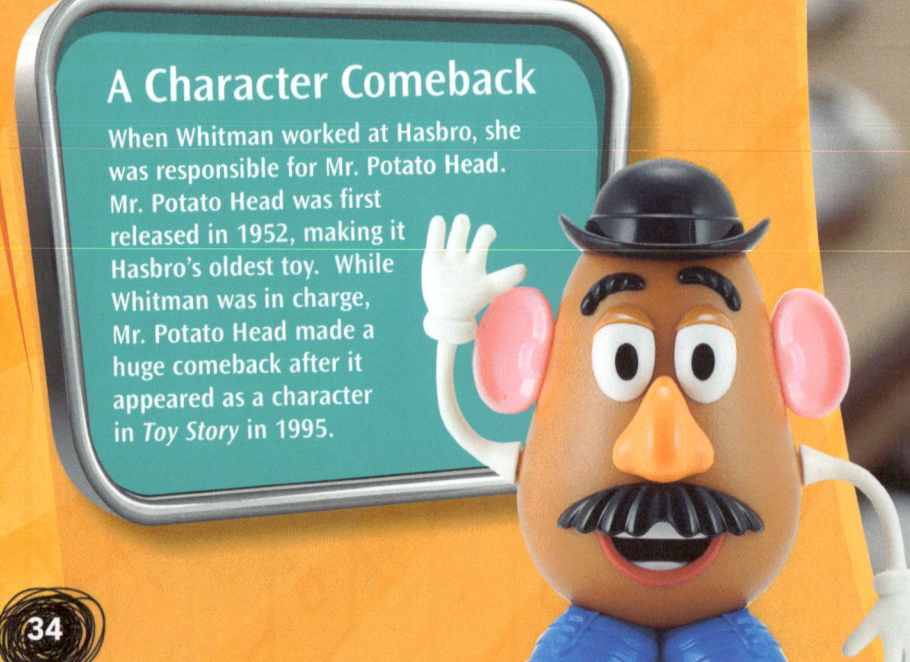

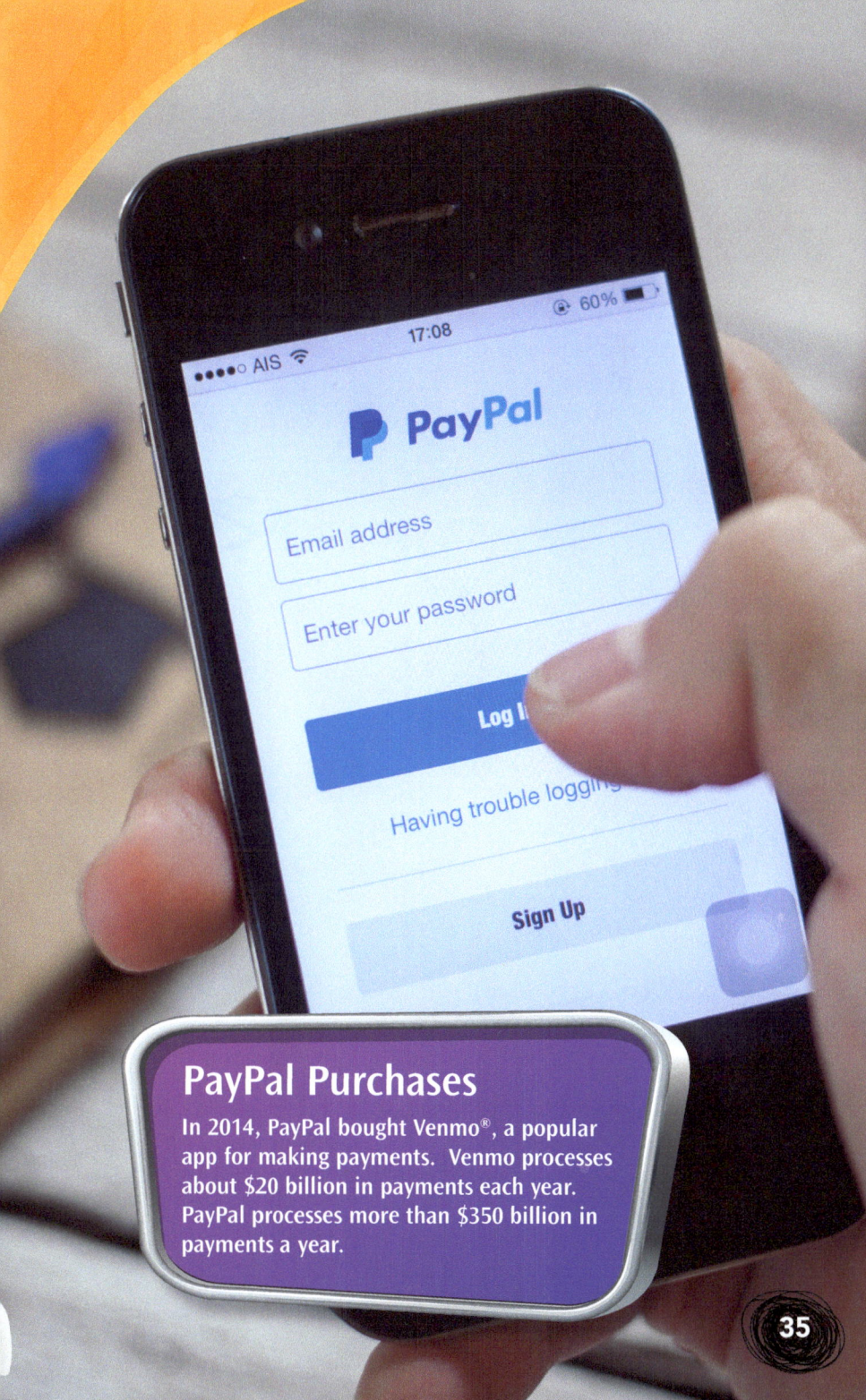

PayPal Purchases

In 2014, PayPal bought Venmo®, a popular app for making payments. Venmo processes about $20 billion in payments each year. PayPal processes more than $350 billion in payments a year.

35

Political Prospect

In 2010, Meg Whitman ran for governor of California. Whitman paid for most of her campaign with her own money, spending a total of $144 million! She lost the governor's race to Jerry Brown.

Under Whitman's leadership, eBay bought Skype® in 2005. Skype users make phone and video calls over the internet. Whitman believed it was important to have each company—eBay, PayPal, and Skype—succeed on its own while also supporting the others. For example, PayPal supports eBay since it has become the most commonly used payment method for eBay.

Whitman's leadership and ideas proved successful for eBay. She left the company in 2008. By that time, there were 15,000 employees. The company earned $8 billion that year. When she left eBay, Whitman was a billionaire and one of the most successful women in the United States.

Whitman successfully transformed eBay and changed the way people buy and sell goods. Now other online marketplaces, such as Etsy® and Poshmark®, sell goods too. Without Whitman's leadership, these types of websites might not exist today.

Whitman's Next Venture

In 2011, Whitman was named CEO of Hewlett-Packard. The company has been around for over 70 years and makes printers, computers, and computer servers. When Whitman took over, the company's sales had declined for many years, but she turned the company around. Within five years, Hewlett-Packard was making money again.

Making Money

There are huge differences between what the average person in the United States earns and what the top business leaders earn. As of 2016, the **median** household income in the United States was $59,039.

In that same year, 12.7 percent of people in the United States were living at or below the poverty line. The poverty line is defined as a yearly income of $24,563 or less for a family of four. In contrast, the average income for the top 5 percent of people in the United States is $225,252. The graph shows the differences in income in the United States.

$24,563	$59,039	$225,252
Poverty	Median	Top 5%

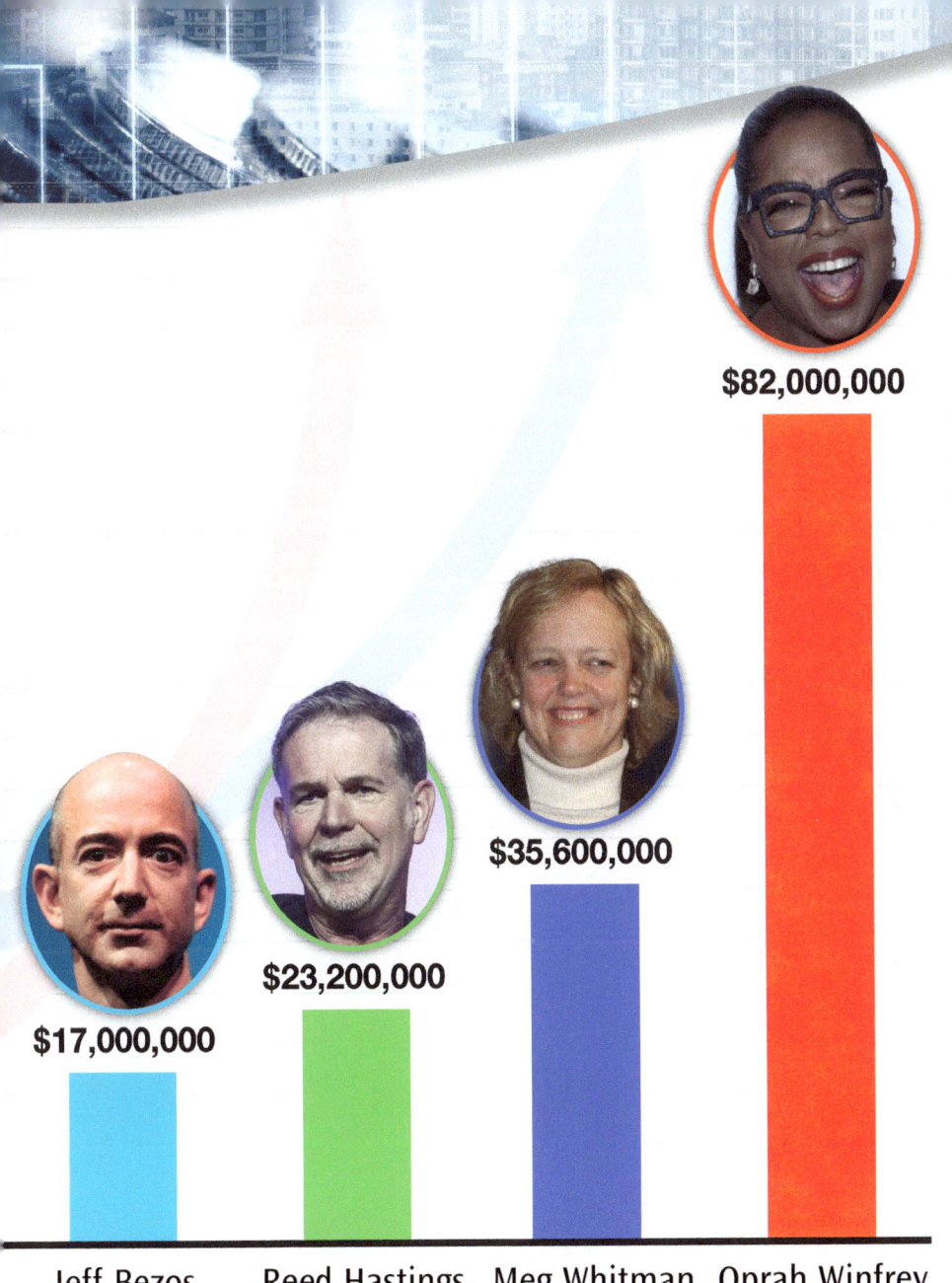

Beyond the Boardroom

Many leaders have changed the way we do or see things. Beyond their business lives, some of the most successful leaders have changed the world in other ways, too. They give their time and money to help people and causes. In 2012 alone, Winfrey gave $400 million to educational causes. Brin has donated $160 million to funding research on Parkinson's disease, a disease that attacks people's nervous systems. Bezos has given millions to health research and education.

Bill and Melinda Gates with Warren Buffett (right)

Sharing Their Wealth

Mark Zuckerberg, the creator of Facebook®, and his wife, Priscilla Chan, have signed the Giving Pledge. They have pledged to give away 99 percent of their net worth throughout their lives. Based on their average net worth, they will end up giving away about $45 billion during their lives.

In 2010, Bill and Melinda Gates and Warren Buffett started the Giving Pledge. They have promised to donate a large portion of their money to causes and to people in need. The Gates and Buffett challenged other billionaires to pledge money, too. As of 2017, there are over 150 people who have promised to give money. These men and women have changed the world through their inventions and leadership and continue to go above and beyond to make the world a better place.

Glossary

accessible—able to be used or obtained

anchor—someone who reads the news on television

bankruptcy—a situation in which a company does not have enough money to pay its debts

brick-and-mortar—a traditional business or store that is in a building instead of on the internet

broadcasting—relating to a radio or television program

chief executive officer—the person who usually has the most authority in a business or organization

commerce—activities that relate to the buying and selling of goods and services

data—information and facts that are usually used to analyze, plan, or calculate something

efficient—capable of producing the desired results without wasting energy, materials, or time

empowering—giving power to someone

gross profits—the total sales of a person or company minus the cost of goods

industry—a group of businesses that work to provide a particular product or service

influential—having power over someone or something to cause change

innovative—having new ideas, inventions, discoveries, or processes for how something can be done

investment firms—companies that invest in and sell shares of other companies

licensed—gave permission to someone to have, show, or do something

median—the middle value in a series of values that have been arranged from smallest to largest

net worth—the value of everything a person or company owns minus all of their debts

on-demand streaming—media that is always available to be played over the internet

personalities—famous people

relevant—closely connected or appropriate to what is being discussed or done

resigned—officially gave up a position or job

revolutionary—causing or relating to a great change

sensitive—likely to cause people to become emotional

subscribers—people who pay money to get a service or publication regularly

syndication—describes a television or radio program that has been sold to many different stations to air as reruns

trailblazer—a person who discovers, makes, or does something new that becomes acceptable or popular

World Wide Web—abbreviated as *www*; the part of the internet that allows people to use browsers to look at websites

Index

Alphabet, 24
Amazon (river), 28
Amazon (website), 4, 15, 28, 30–32
AM Chicago, 7
Apple: Computers, 16, 19; I, 19; Inc., 19–21, 23; iPad, 17, 20; iPhone, 20–21; iPod, 19–20; iTunes, 20; iTunes Store, 20; Pay, 20; TV, 20; Watch, 20
AuctionWeb, 32–33
Backrub, 22
Beanie Baby, 32
Bezos, Jeff, 28–32, 39–40
Blockbuster Video, 12–13
Blue Origin, 29
Brin, Sergey, 22–27, 40
Brown, Jerry, 36
Buffett, Warren, 30, 41
Cadabra, 28
California, 23, 32, 36
California State Board of Education, 14
Chan, Priscilla, 41

Cook, Tim, 20–21
Donahue, 7
eBay, 4, 32–34, 37
Etsy, 37
Facebook, 41
Forbes (magazine), 30
Gates, Bill, 30, 41
Gates, Melinda, 41
Giving Pledge, 41
Google: website, 4, 22–27; Earth, 27; Glass, 25; Maps, 26; X, 25
Googlebot, 23
Harpo Studios, 9
Harvard University, 34
Hasbro, 34
Hastings, Reed, 12–14, 39
Hewlett-Packard, 37
Hulu, 15
Jobs, Steve, 16, 18–21
koumpounophobia, 18
Massachusetts, 34
Microsoft, 30
Mr. Potato Head, 34

Netflix, 13–15
New Jersey, 34
New York City, 28
NeXT, 19
Omidyar, Pierre, 32–33
O magazine, 11
Oprah's Angel Network, 10
Oprah's Book Club, 9
Oprah Winfrey Network (OWN), 10
Oprah Winfrey Show, The, 6, 9–11
Page, Larry, 22–24, 26–27
PageRank, 24
PayPal, 34–35, 37
Pixar Animation Studios, 18
Poshmark, 37
Prime Air, 32
Princeton University, 34
San Jose, California, 32
Schiller, Phil, 21

Seattle, Washington, 28
Skype, 37
Stanford University, 23
Toy Story, 19, 34
Universal Automatic Computer (UNIVAC), 16–17
Venmo, 35
Wall Street, 28
Wal-Mart, 8
Walton, Alice, 8
Walton, Sam, 8
Whitman, Meg, 32–34, 36–37, 39
Whole Foods, 30
Winfrey, Oprah, 6–11, 39–40
World Wide Web, 23, 28
Wozniak, Steve "the Woz", 16
YouTube, 15
Zuckerberg, Mark, 41

Check It Out!

Books

Blumenthal, Karen. 2012. *Steve Jobs: The Man Who Thought Different: A Biography*. New York: Square Fish.

Bjergegaard, Martin, and Cosmina Popa. 2016. *How to Be a Leader*. New York: The School of Life.

Videos

GeekWire. "Jeff Bezos speaks with students at the opening of the Apollo exhibit at The Museum of Flight."

The School of Life. "How to Be an Entrepreneur."

Websites

Entrepreneur. *Young Entrepreneurs*. www.entrepreneur.com/topic/young-entrepreneurs.

Google. *Doodles*. www.google.com/doodles.

Forbes. *Forbes Under 30*. www.forbes.com/under30.

Try It!

There are numerous business leaders who have changed the world, many of whom are not named in this book. Pick one business leader who you think should be added to this book. Write a chapter (two to three pages) about this person and the ways he or she has changed the world.

- Research information about your business leader. Find information about how he or she has changed the way in which we view the world.

- Locate at least two "fun facts" about this person. Use those facts to write two sidebars in your chapter.

- Find images to support the information in your chapter. Be sure to write a caption for each image you use.

- Lay out your information and images into a chapter. You can use paper and photos or organize your chapter digitally.

- Share your chapter with friends and family so they can learn more about the leader you selected.

About the Author

Kristy Stark has written books about everything from the history of telephones to the game of Quidditch. When she is not busy writing, she enjoys running, reading, and doing just about anything outdoors. Most of all, she loves to spend time with her husband and two young children. They love to go swimming, hiking, and camping in the warm California sun.

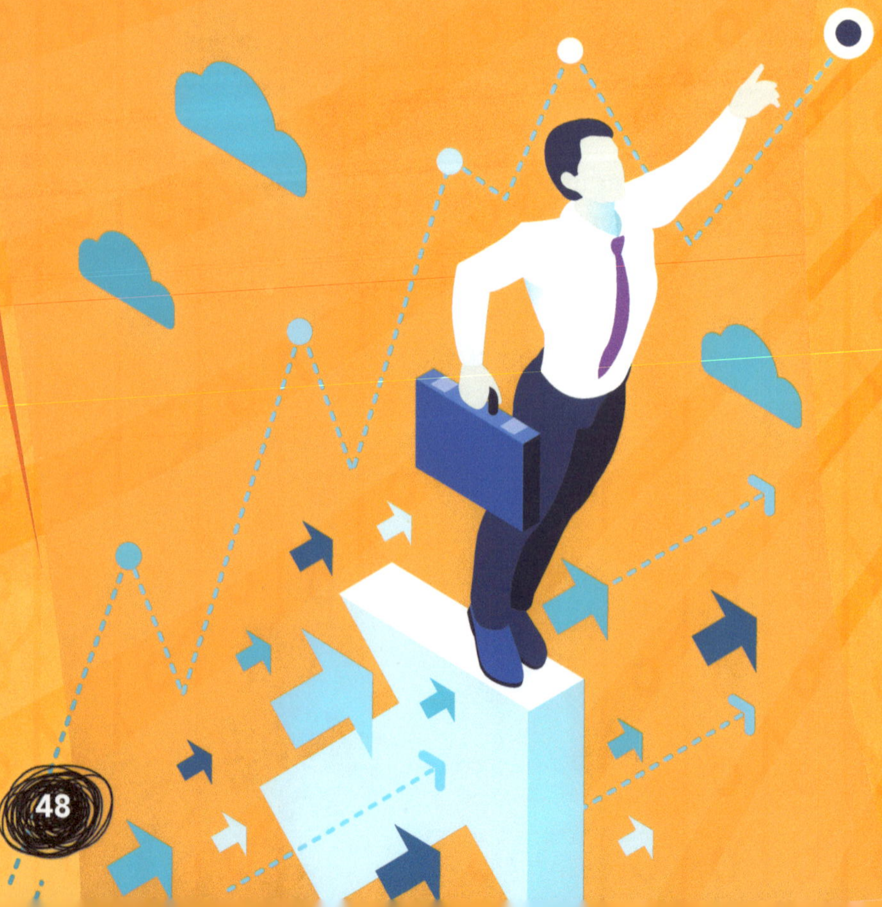

www.ingramcontent.com/pod-product-compliance
Lightning Source LLC
Chambersburg PA
CBHW041505010526
44118CB00001B/26